Written by James Clements and Jo Nelson
With additional material by Tom Evans

PUFFIN BOOKS

UK | USA | Canada | Ireland | Australia
India | New Zealand | South Africa

Puffin Books is part of the Penguin Random House group of companies
whose addresses can be found at global.penguinrandomhouse.com.
www.penguin.co.uk   www.puffin.co.uk   www.ladybird.co.uk

Roald Dahl quotations from *The Twits* (1980, 2022), *Matilda* (1988, 2023), *James and the Giant Peach* (1961, 2022) and *Charlie and the Chocolate Factory* (1964, 2022). All titles are published by Puffin Books.
Selected material from *Roald Dahl Creative Writing with The Twits: Remarkable Reasons to Write* (2020), *Roald Dahl Creative Writing with Charlie and the Chocolate Factory: How to Write Tremendous Characters* (2019), *Roald Dahl Creative Writing with Matilda: How to Write Spellbinding Speech* (2019) and *Roald Dahl Creative Writing with Fantastic Mr Fox: How to Write a Marvellous Plot* (2020), all published by Puffin Books.
First published 2026
001

Text copyright © The Roald Dahl Story Company Ltd, 2026
Illustrations copyright © Quentin Blake, 2026
ROALD DAHL is a registered trademark of The Roald Dahl Story Company Ltd.

www.roalddahl.com

The moral right of Roald Dahl and Quentin Blake has been asserted

Penguin Random House values and supports copyright. Copyright fuels creativity, encourages diverse voices, promotes freedom of expression and supports a vibrant culture. Thank you for purchasing an authorized edition of this book and for respecting intellectual property laws by not reproducing, scanning or distributing any part of it by any means without permission. You are supporting authors and enabling Penguin Random House to continue to publish books for everyone. No part of this book may be used or reproduced in any manner for the purpose of training artificial intelligence technologies or systems. In accordance with Article 4(3) of the DSM Directive 2019/790, Penguin Random House expressly reserves this work from the text and data mining exception.

Printed in China

The authorized representative in the EEA is Penguin Random House Ireland,
Morrison Chambers, 32 Nassau Street, Dublin D02 YH68

A CIP catalogue record for this book is available from the British Library

ISBN: 978-0-241-61079-4

All correspondence to:
Puffin Books
Penguin Random House Children's
One Embassy Gardens, 8 Viaduct Gardens, London SW11 7BW

Roald Dahl

How to Be a Writer

SWASHBOGGLING NON-FICTION

CONTENTS

How to use this book — 6

Reasons to write — 8

Exciting non-fiction — 12

Not just facts — 16

"You wanted cake!" — 20

Letters and notes — 24

Dear Diary — 28

Super stories — 32

Interesting instructions — 36

Ridiculous recipes — 40

Powerful persuasion — 44

"I don't want a grown-up person" — 48

Amazing adverts — 52

Hopscotchy speech marks — 56

He said, she said	60
Read all about it!	64
Questions and answers	68
Incredible interviews	72
Perfect play-scripts	76
Through each other's eyes	80
You are a writer!	84
Time to plan your writing!	86
My remarkable reasons to write	88

HOW TO USE THIS BOOK

In this book, you will practise writing to entertain, inform and persuade. You will learn how to write exciting interviews, play-scripts, diary entries, recipes, instructions and more. Anyone can be a writer, so grab your pen and have fun!

Make sure you have the following things before you start: pens, pencils and an eraser. If you have a dictionary and a thesaurus, they will come in handy, too.

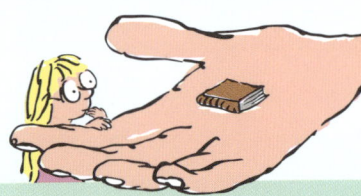

As you go through this book, look out for lots of tips, tricks and fun ideas that will help you along the way.

Remember, different types of writing have their own rules. Learning these can help you to shape your writing.

Think about the audience you are writing for and the purpose of your writing before you start. This will help you to think about what you need to write.

Sometimes you need to write using a formal tone, while other times your writing will be informal.

Some types of writing can provide you with a great way of starting a story or thinking more deeply about an idea. You can use interviews to think about how your characters speak, or play-scripts to plan a piece of dialogue.

You can use different types of writing within a story to add some excitement or to explain something to your reader.

Reread your work, and imagine you are the reader.
Would you know what was going on?
Would you understand the topic clearly?

Remember that it is possible to overuse certain features and effects in your writing. If you use a feature too often, it stops having such a special effect.

You don't always have to stick to the rules for different types of writing. You are the author! Have fun mixing different writing features, and see if it helps you to share an idea with your reader.

Whatever your reason to write, make sure you have fun!

Stay safe online! Some of the activities in this book ask you to do some research. If you do any of your research online, remember:

- ask an adult to help
- use well-known search engines, such as Google or Kiddle
- never share personal details, such as your name, home or school address, phone number or photos.

REASONS TO WRITE

People write for lots of different reasons. For example, a newspaper article is written to tell us what is happening, a play-script is written for actors to perform, and a recipe book explains how to cook delicious food.

This disgusting description of beards at the beginning of *The Twits* has been written because the writer wants the reader to see things from his point of view. Can you think of some reasons why you like to write?

> Things cling to hairs, especially food. Things like gravy go right in among the hairs and stay there. You and I can wipe our smooth faces with a flannel . . . but the hairy man cannot do that.

What makes you want to read a story or watch a film? Have a think about some of your favourite books, films and games. On a piece of paper, write down how they make you feel.

Think about the types of writing that you do. Put a tick next to each one to show how often you do it.

WHAT KIND OF WRITER ARE YOU?

QUIZ

	At home			At school		
	never	sometimes	often	never	sometimes	often
story	☐	☐	☐	☐	☐	☐
letter	☐	☐	☐	☐	☐	☐
diary entry	☐	☐	☐	☐	☐	☐
email	☐	☐	☐	☐	☐	☐
notes	☐	☐	☐	☐	☐	☐
instructions	☐	☐	☐	☐	☐	☐
poem	☐	☐	☐	☐	☐	☐
list	☐	☐	☐	☐	☐	☐
text message	☐	☐	☐	☐	☐	☐
recipe	☐	☐	☐	☐	☐	☐
report	☐	☐	☐	☐	☐	☐
newspaper article	☐	☐	☐	☐	☐	☐

Don't worry if there are some kinds of writing you haven't tried yet. This book is here to help!

When you write, think about the audience (who you're writing for) and the purpose (why you're writing). This will help you to decide what to write and how to write it.

Match each type of writing to its audience.

An advert for football boots					Evie, age 4

Mrs Twit's diary					Chris, the owner of 'Vegetarian Dining'

The Friendly Puppy picture book					Emma, a team captain

A recipe for turnip pie					Mrs Twit

Reasons to read

Look at the types of writing listed below. Who do you think might read each one and why?

- A cereal box
- A magazine about cats
- A book of fairy tales
- The instructions for a new board game
- The biography of a famous singer
- A newspaper article about an election

Some types of writing can sound very different from others. Match the sentences below to the types of writing they come from.

Slowly, Leila crept across the garden.	letter
HUGTIGHT: The stickiest glue in the world!	newspaper article
1. First, take one large pie tin.	recipe
MONKEYS RUN FREE!	advert
Dear Mr Twit,	story

How could you tell the types of writing apart?

letter

newspaper article

recipe

advert

story

EXCITING NON-FICTION

Non-fiction is writing that is about real life. It often gives us information about a real-life subject. You might find non-fiction writing in a book, a magazine or online.

Read the sentences about birds below. Circle any that come from non-fiction writing.

Once upon a time, an amazing, invisible bird hatched out of an enormous egg.

Some scientists believe that birds evolved from dinosaurs.

"It must be berries," sang the Roly-Poly Bird.

Penguins have special waterproof feathers to keep them dry as they swim underwater.

All birds hatch from eggs.

Great non-fiction writing is clear and easy to follow, but is still written in an interesting way. Look at how these facts about parrots have been turned into a fun paragraph of non-fiction writing.

- Parrots are intelligent.
- They have strong beaks for crushing nuts and seeds.
- Many types of parrots live in rainforests.
- Most live in big groups.
- Many make a lot of noise.

One of the cleverest species of bird, parrots often live in huge, noisy families. They can be found in rainforests all over the world. They love to munch on nuts and seeds, and they use their powerful beaks to break open the shells.

It's your turn to be a fact-finder! Research an animal or a person. Make a note of the information you find and use it to write a paragraph that draws the reader in. Use the ideas box for extra help.

Ideas box

crocodiles

giraffes

an inventor

a grandparent

Think of a topic you really care about, and do some research on it. Note down some of the facts you would like to tell a reader about this topic. Use the ideas box for extra help.

Topic: _____

Ideas box

your favourite game	where you live	looking after our planet
an animal you like	your favourite sports team	a fun place you have visited
your pet	your family	a science topic

Now try writing your facts as an interesting piece of non-fiction.

Do your research! If you are writing non-fiction, everything you write needs to be true and accurate. You can't just write any old thing!

NOT JUST FACTS

Good non-fiction writing is more than just a list of facts. Here are some ways that you can write exciting non-fiction to really grip your reader.

Sometimes a writer will talk directly to the reader using words like "you" or "us". Read this example from *The Twits*.

*What a lot of hairy-faced men there are around nowadays . . .
So what I want to know is this. How often do all these
hairy-faced men wash their faces? Is it only once a week, like us,
on Sunday nights? And do they shampoo it? Do they use a hairdryer?
Do they rub hair tonic in to stop their faces from going bald?*

Pick a topic, and finish the sentences below with facts about your topic.

You have probably heard of _____

_____.

It is important for us to _____

_____.

One thing you might not know is _____

_____.

You won't believe it, but _____

_____.

You can also use rhetorical questions. These are questions that a writer asks but doesn't expect you to answer. Finish the questions below with more facts on your topic from page 16.

Can you think of _____

_____ ?

Did you know that _____

_____ ?

Have you ever wondered why _____

_____ ?

Can you imagine _____

_____ ?

Rhetorical questions work best if you use them carefully and not too often.

This is a diagram of Mr Twit's beard. Drawings and diagrams can also be used in non-fiction. Draw a diagram to go with your non-fiction writing from pages 16 and 17. Don't forget to label your drawing.

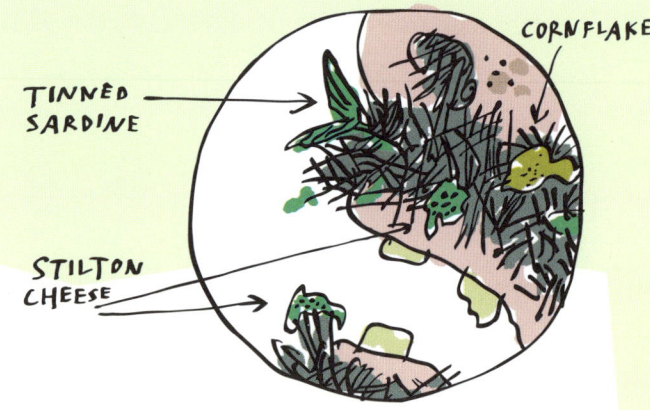

Write your own non-fiction text. You can carry on writing about the topic you chose on page 16, or pick a completely new topic! Use the ideas box for extra help.

Try writing your facts in ways the reader might not expect. You could write them as a poem, a joke or a speech.

Ideas box

interesting facts for the reader

clear sentences

rhetorical questions

talking to the reader using "you"

drawings or diagrams

Read back over your writing, and imagine that you are someone who doesn't know anything about the topic. Does it make sense? Can you make it clearer?

"YOU WANTED CAKE!"

There are four main sentence types. These are: statements, questions, commands and exclamations.

Read these examples from *Matilda*.

Statements give a fact or an opinion. They usually end with a full stop.

"No one ever got rich being honest," the father said.

Exclamations show strong feelings. They usually end with an exclamation mark.

"You're just an ignorant little squirt who hasn't the foggiest idea what you're talking about!"

Questions ask something. They always end with a question mark.

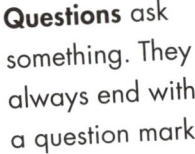

"Can you really turn the mileage back with an electric drill?" young Michael asked.

Commands instruct someone to do something. They usually end with a full stop.

"I'm telling you trade secrets," the father said. "So don't you go talking about this to anyone else."

Tick to show whether each quote is a statement, question, command or exclamation.

	statement	question	command	exclamation
"I'll give you pigtails, you little rat!"				
"Spell cat, Nigel."				
"This is Matilda's teacher."				
"Where are the children's books, please?"				
"Never argue with her."				
"These drills run at tremendous speed."				

Now come up with a statement, a question, a command and an exclamation of your own.

Statements and questions are used a lot in speech. Imagine one person has been to the beach and another person wants to hear all about it. Write their conversation below, using statements and questions.

When you're writing speech, you don't always need to use long sentences. Sometimes "Really?" or "Oh no!" helps to make the conversation believable.

In *Matilda*, Miss Trunchbull commands Bruce Bogtrotter to eat an entire chocolate cake in front of the whole school. Think about what Bruce might want to say to her, then write it here, using lots of exclamations.

"Eat!" she shouted, banging her thigh with the riding crop. "If I tell you to eat, you will eat! You wanted cake! You stole cake! And now you've got cake! What's more, you're going to eat it! You do not leave this platform and nobody leaves this hall until you have eaten the entire cake that is sitting there in front of you!"

Check your work

Have these sentences been written correctly? Write the corrections on a piece of paper.

- "Stop that at once?"
- Did you know that Oompa-Loompas love cheese!
- "Hooray. Yippee. Wahoo." Mr Fox cried.
- This, whispered the BFG, "is the most delumptious Frobscottle ever?"

LETTERS AND NOTES

People write letters and notes for lots of different reasons. A letter or note might be written on paper and posted, or typed and sent as an email. Some are very serious and formal, while others are very informal.

Mr Twit has received two letters. Are they formal or informal?

HUGTIGHT Glue Co.
London,
England

Dear Mr Twit,

It has come to our attention that you have been using our patented HUGTIGHT glue to catch birds in your garden.

We are writing to ask you to stop this beastly practice immediately.

Yours sincerely,

Ms L. Stickitt
Manager, HUGTIGHT Glue Co.

Formal: ☐   **Informal:** ☐

Hello, you grizzly old grunion,

Hope you enjoyed the wormy spaghetti! I've got another "treat" planned for your dinner tonight. Ha! Ha!

From,

Mrs Twit

Formal: ☐   **Informal:** ☐

Formal letters often begin with "Dear", and end with "Yours sincerely" or "Yours faithfully". Informal letters sound more like speech. Look again at the two letters, and underline formal features in blue and informal features in red.

Secret messages

Want to pass secret letters to your friends and family? Try writing in invisible ink! All you need is some paper and lemon juice. Write the message with the juice, then leave it to dry. Tell your friend to put the message somewhere warm and the secret message will appear!

Even secret-er messages

Has your lemon-juice scheme been rumbled? Come up with a code! You could try swapping letters of the alphabet or replacing them with numbers.

Write two letters to Mrs Twit. One should be formal, and the other should be informal. Think about who is writing to Mrs Twit and what they want to say to her. Include some of the features from pages 24 and 25. Use the ideas box for extra help.

Informal letter:

Ideas box

Who could write to Mrs Twit?

- a cooking magazine
- a doctor
- a company that sells windows
- Mr Twit
- the Roly-Poly Bird

Formal letter:

> If you begin a formal letter with "Dear" and someone's name, you should end it with "Yours sincerely". If you don't address them by name, you should end with "Yours faithfully".

Formal or informal?

If you had to write letters to these people, do you think you would use informal language?

- Your best friend
- A king
- Your teacher
- Your sibling

Letter-writing checklist

Does your formal letter have:
- [ ] an address?
- [ ] the date?
- [ ] the right kind of greeting?
- [ ] the right kind of sign-off?
- [ ] your signature?

DEAR DIARY

People who keep diaries or journals write in them every day about the things they do or the way they feel. In most types of writing, we think carefully about the audience, but in diaries or journals people are writing just for themselves.

Do you keep a diary or write in a journal? What do you write about, or what would you write about if you did? Think about things that have happened that you'd like to remember, and write them in the space below.

Diary entries are written in the first person. In the first person, writers use "I" and "me" to talk about themselves or their character. Read the sentences below. Circle the sentences that are written in the first person.

The princess enjoyed the party so much.

I met Aunt Sponge and Aunt Spiker today, and I didn't like them at all.

Today, they went out for lunch.

My brother and I went to the cinema.

You'll never believe what happened to me today!

I told them I'm a short-horned grasshopper.

If you are writing a diary entry as a character, you need to describe their feelings. Look carefully at the pictures below. What adjectives, or describing words, could you use to describe how James and his aunts, Aunt Spiker and Aunt Sponge, feel?

Read the story text below.

The two women and the small boy stood absolutely still on the grass underneath the tree, gazing up at this extraordinary fruit. James's little face was glowing with excitement, his eyes were as big and bright as two stars. He could see the peach swelling larger and larger as clearly as if it were a balloon being blown up. In half a minute, it was the size of a melon!
In another half-minute, it was twice as big again!

Write a diary entry for James on the day he sees the giant peach.

Dear Diary,
You won't believe what I saw today!

You don't have to write about *everything* that happened that day in a diary, just the bits you remember best. If you can remember it, that's what's worth recording in your diary!

Dahl diaries

Have a think about these other characters from stories written by Roald Dahl, and the events within those stories. What might they write about in their diaries?

- When Matilda meets Miss Honey for the first time
- When the Duke sees the Giraffe, the Pelly, the Monkey and the boy arrive to clean his windows
- When the BFG is given an elephant

Choose your favourite, and write their diary entry for that day.

SUPER STORIES

Stories are descriptions of events and people. They can be made up, or they can be based on or report real events (narrative non-fiction). You can tell a story to share a message or just entertain. But stories should always be interesting!

Some stories have a message for the reader. In *Matilda*, there is one dreadful character – Miss Trunchbull, the Head Teacher.

There was an aura of menace about her even at a distance, and when she came up close you could almost feel the dangerous heat radiating from her as from a red-hot rod of metal. When she marched – Miss Trunchbull never walked, she always marched like a storm trooper with long strides and arms a-swinging – when she marched along a corridor you could actually hear her snorting as she went, and if a group of children happened to be in her path, she ploughed right on through them like a tank, with small people bouncing off her to left and right.

Why do you think Miss Trunchbull is described like this?

What message does the description send to the reader?

Whether your story is as short as a Minpin or longer than the BFG, it needs some characters! Think about a story you could write, and make notes in the spaces below.

The hero of the story
(also called the "protagonist")

The big bad villain
(also called the "antagonist")

The characters your hero meets

What your hero wants to achieve

How the villain gets in the hero's way

Remember, you can make interesting things happen to your characters. They will have to make choices, and those choices have consequences!

Here are two story starters. Write the next part of each story in a way that makes the reader want to read on!

The rain was pouring and the children had been inside all day. Just then,

The animals of the forest all lived together. One day,

Short and sweet

Can you write a story in just:

- 100 words?
- 50 words?
- 20 words?

Now think about how you can engage your reader while writing narrative non-fiction. Think of incredible events or people you've heard about. Use the ideas box below for extra help. Use the questions below to plan a story about them.

Why not pick one of your ideas from pages 33–35 and write the whole story?

Who or what is your story about?

Where is it set?

What happens at the beginning?

What happens at the end?

Ideas box

a person from history

the first person to...

a famous person

an incredibly unlikely event

a moment in history

an invention that changed the world

What could other people learn from this story?

INTERESTING INSTRUCTIONS

Instructions are written to tell people how to do something. They need to be clear and simple so the reader can understand them easily.

Read Mr Twit's instructions on how to catch birds for Bird Pie.

Catching birds

You will need:

- one ladder
- one Big Dead Tree
- one paintbrush
- one tin of HUGTIGHT glue

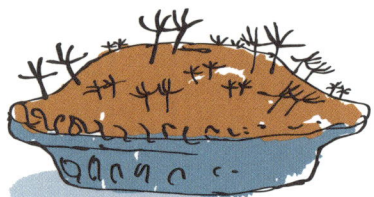

You could use a set of instructions in one of your stories. Perhaps your characters find the instructions for a time machine, or they need the missing instructions to deactivate a rocket!

Use Mr Twit's instructions on the opposite page to fill in the first four gaps in the instructions below. Then work out which word belongs in the last gap, and fill it in.

Instructions:

1. First, use the _____ to climb into the branches of the Big Dead Tree.

2. Using a _____, cover the branches of the Big Dead Tree in HUGTIGHT glue.

3. Then climb down, leaving the branches covered in lots of sticky _____.

4. At sundown, watch as birds fly to roost in the _____.

5. Finally, return the next morning and grab all of the _____ that are stuck to the branches.

Other instructions

There are lots of different kinds of instructions you could try writing. For example, you could try to:

- give directions to Giant Country
- explain how to mix chocolate by waterfall
- explain how to make breakfast as a mouse.

Instructions often use command sentences to tell the reader what to do. It is important to choose the right verb, or doing word, so the instructions are easy to follow.

Mr Twit is giving some instructions to Muggle-Wump the monkey and his family. They are in the Great Upside-Down Monkey Circus. Read the command sentences, then add the missing verbs.

_____ to the music upside down!

_____ a football upside down!

_____ your food upside down!

_____ your water upside down!

"Attention!" he barked in his fearsome monkey-trainer's voice. "Upside down, all of you and jump to it! One on top of the other! Quick! Get on with it or you'll feel Mrs Twit's stick across your backsides!"

Imagine Muggle-Wump wants to play a trick on Mr Twit. Write the instructions for the trick below. Use the ideas box for extra help.

Ideas box

Tell the reader what to do and how to do it.

Use clear language.

Write the instructions in numbered steps.

Show what order to do things in (first, next).

Choose your verbs carefully (collect, balance, hide).

Read back over your instructions, and check them carefully. Are all the steps there? Do any of the steps need to be clearer?

RIDICULOUS RECIPES

Recipes are a special type of instruction. They tell people how to cook and prepare different types of food and drink. It is important for recipes to be very clear, so the food tastes good at the end!

Recipes normally start with a list of ingredients, or the things you need to put in the dish. Finish the list of ingredients for your own sweet treat inspired by *Charlie and the Chocolate Factory*. Use the instructions on the opposite page for ideas.

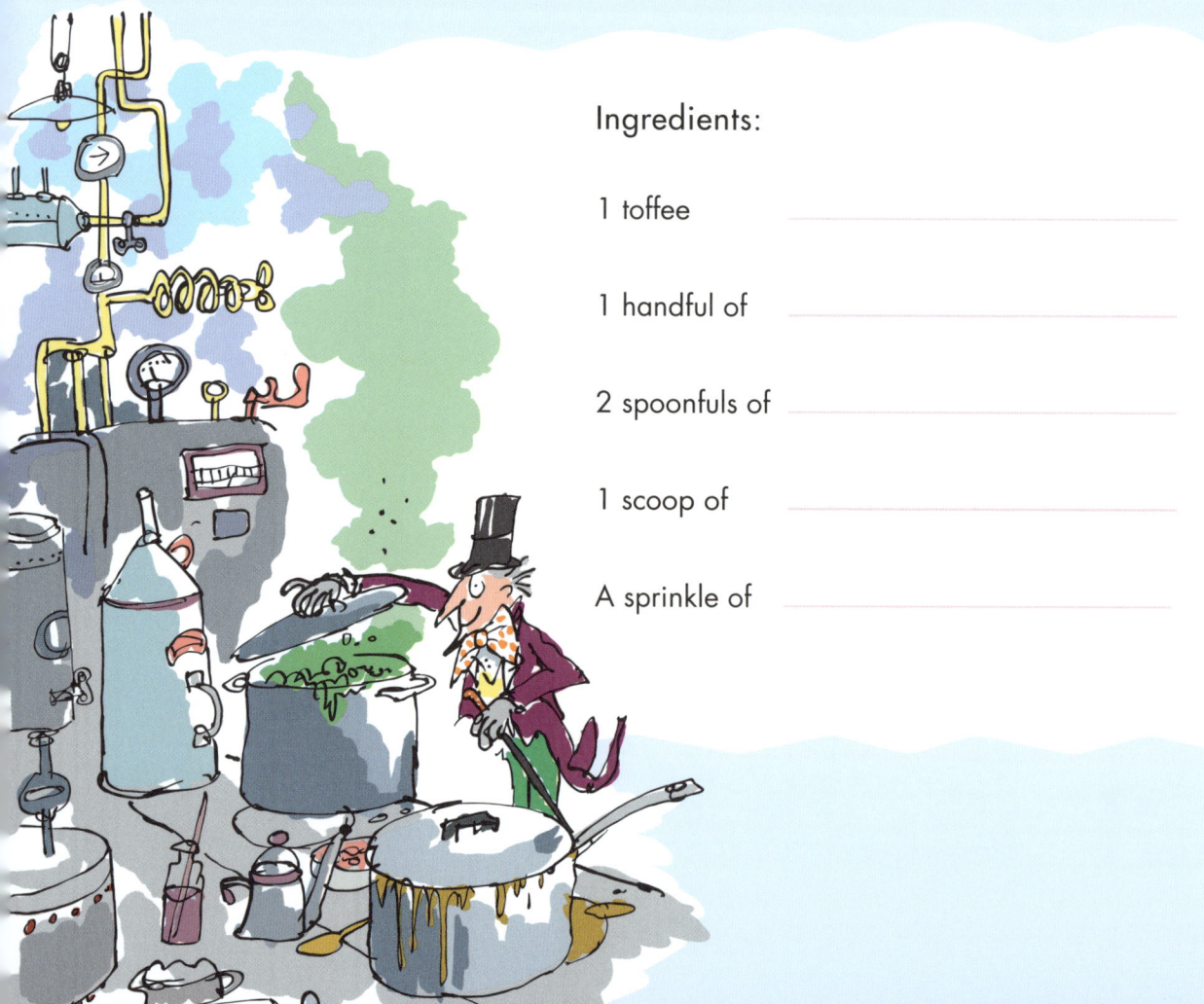

Ingredients:

1 toffee _____

1 handful of _____

2 spoonfuls of _____

1 scoop of _____

A sprinkle of _____

Choose words to fill in the gaps below. Use the ideas box for extra help.

1. _____, pick one toffee apple from your toffee-apple tree.

2. _____, chop the toffee apple.

3. _____, mix with snozzberries in a pan.

4. _____, add to the mixture and put in the fridge until _____.

5. _____, serve in a _____ with ice cream and decorate with _____.

Ideas box

Next	First	cooled	coconut
Finally	After that	bowl	sweets
Then	Lastly	teacup	honey

Roald Dahl's books are full of weird and wonderful meals you could make up and write imaginary recipes for. For example, there's:

- the BFG's Frobscottle
- the Centipede's Scrambled Dregs and Stinkbug Eggs
- Willy Wonka's lickable wallpaper!

See what fantabulous foods you can find!

Think of a tasty invention for Willy Wonka to make. Use the words below to help you write your recipe for it.

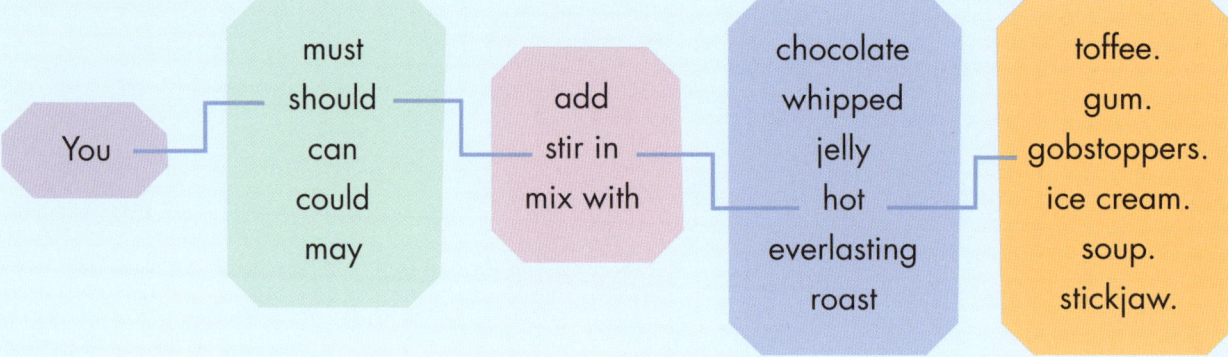

Home cooking

Ask your grown-ups if you can help them to make a meal or do some baking. As you go, write down all the instructions they give you to turn the ingredients into a tasty dish!

What new recipe would you invent if Willy Wonka gave the chocolate factory to you? Write it down below.

Recipe: _____

Ingredients:

-
-
-
-
-

Instructions:

1. First,

2.

3.

4.

5.

Cookbook compilation

If you enjoy writing recipes, why not try collecting lots of them together, and making your own cookbook?

POWERFUL PERSUASION

Persuasive writing tries to make the reader agree with the writer's point of view. You can find persuasive language in magazine articles, letters and adverts.

If you were writing to persuade Mr Twit to let the monkeys go free, you might use:

Logic and facts
In the wild, monkeys travel long distances. Keeping monkeys in small cages can give them health problems.

Emotion
It is unkind to keep the monkeys locked up! How would you feel if you were them?

Consequences
Do you have a licence to keep monkeys, Mr Twit? I will report you to the police.

Plan a persuasive argument of your own. Think carefully about who you are trying to persuade and why. Use the ideas box for extra help.

Ideas box

Mrs Twit should stop making Bird Pie.

You should be allowed to stay up later at night.

Your sibling should share their books with you.

Muggle-Wump the monkey should plan an escape from the Twits' garden.

I am writing to persuade _____

to _____
_____.

| Logic and facts | Emotion | Consequences |

Now write your persuasive argument.

When trying to persuade someone, use powerful describing words.

45

Conjunctions link two words or phrases together. You can use conjunctions to build a persuasive argument. Choose a conjunction for each sentence below, then finish the sentences. Use the ideas box for extra help.

Muggle-Wump and his family are unhappy _____

The monkeys' cage is too small _____

You might enjoy training monkeys _____

Ideas box

and	which
but	since
or	until
because	while
if	although
unless	that

Persuade me!

Write these opinions down on a piece of paper. Then write persuasive arguments around them in a different colour. You can choose to agree with the opinions or try to change the writer's mind.

- "Children should be seen but not heard!"
- "Mr Fickelgruber's chocolate is much better than Mr Wonka's!"
- "You could never fly a peach to New York!"

Write a persuasive formal letter using your plan on page 45. Use conjunctions to help structure your argument.

Rhetorical questions (page 17) can be really useful in persuasive writing, too. For example, "How would you feel if . . . ?" See if you can use them here!

Dear _____,

Yours sincerely,

_____

"I DON'T WANT A GROWN-UP PERSON"

You can use persuasive language when you want someone to agree with you.

The children who win Golden Tickets would all like to take over Willy Wonka's chocolate factory. How might these characters use persuasive language to try to convince Willy Wonka that they are the right person for the job?

Augustus Gloop – a greedy boy

"Pick me, Mr Wonka, because _____

_____

_____

_____!"

Veruca Salt – a girl who is spoilt by her parents

"But I want your factory because _____

_____

_____

_____!"

Violet Beauregarde – a girl who chews gum all day long

"No! Pick me because _____
_____
_____
_____!"

> **Ideas box**
> surely
> obviously
> it's clear that
> the best choice
> I believe

Mike Teavee – a boy who does nothing but watch television

"Give your factory to me! I _____
_____
_____
_____!"

"I don't want a grown-up person at all. A grown-up won't listen to me; they won't learn. They will try to do things their own way and not mine. So I have to have a child. I want a good, sensible, loving child, one to whom I can tell all my most precious sweet-making secrets – while I am still alive."

Imagine Willy Wonka has asked children from all over the world to apply for the job. Fill in the application form below. You can be anyone you like – a made-up character, someone you know in real life or yourself.

Willy Wonka's Chocolate Factory

Name: _____

School: _____

What makes you the perfect person to run Willy Wonka's chocolate factory?

_____

_____

_____

What skills do you have that will be useful in this job?

_____

_____

_____

What things have you done in the past that will help you in this job?

_____

_____

_____

What's your best idea for a completely new kind of chocolate or sweet?

_____

_____

_____

Draw a picture of your idea here.

> Remember to use persuasive language. You want to convince Willy Wonka that your character is the right person for the job!

AMAZING ADVERTS

Adverts are usually written to persuade someone to buy something. They can be funny, entertaining or memorable, but they always try to be persuasive.

Many products have a slogan. A slogan is a short phrase that is easy to remember and tells you something about the product. Slogans sometimes include puns, alliteration or rhyme.

Pun

A play on words, where the sentence can have two meanings

HUGTIGHT Glue
You'll be pleased you stuck with HUGTIGHT.

Alliteration

Words that have the same first sound and are close together

Sara's Spaghetti
Splendid spaghetti for special suppers

Rhyme

Words that have the same sounds at the end

GREAT MONKEY CIRCUS
See a monkey – just like a clown, but upside down!

Invent some slogans for these new products. Try to use a pun, alliteration or rhyme in each one.

Mr Twit's Monkey Cages _____

Bubbly Beard Bath _____

Float-away Balloons _____

Mrs Twit's Oven-ready Pies _____

You can use positive adjectives to make your product sound as wonderful as possible. Add some more positive adjectives to the lists below.

delicious	reliable	strong

Buy this!

Use your persuasive language to convince your friends or family to buy something silly from around the house. Try to "sell" them:

- a washing-up sponge
- an alarm clock
- your least favourite teddy
- one sock.

Can you plan an advert for Mrs Twit's Oven-ready Pies? Use some of your adjectives from page 53, and think about the ideas below.

A snappy slogan

Facts about the pie

Rhetorical questions

Emotional argument

Puns, alliteration and rhyme

Now write your advert! Try to make Mrs Twit's pies sound irresistible!

Mrs Twit's Oven-ready Pies

Poster perfection

Once you've written your advert, draw and colour in a poster to put on a wall at home! Use bright, eye-catching colours to draw a picture of Mrs Twit's pies.

HOPSCOTCHY SPEECH MARKS

When you include speech in a non-fiction story or newspaper article, you use inverted commas, like these: " ". They are called speech marks.

"I'm sure it's right," Matilda said.

Speech marks go on either side of the words being said. Can you put the speech marks in the right places? Look at the example from *Matilda* above for extra help.

There it is. Its name is Chopper.

Make it talk.

You can't make it talk. You have to be patient. It'll talk when it feels like it.

Any punctuation, such as a full stop or an exclamation mark, should go inside the speech marks.

Here is the same text again, but this time you can see who is speaking. Can you put speech marks in the right places again?

There it is, Fred said. Its name is Chopper.

Make it talk, Matilda said.

You can't make it talk, Fred said. You have to be patient. It'll talk when it feels like it.

Fred and Matilda are talking about Fred's parrot. Continue their conversation below. What questions could Matilda ask? Remember to use speech marks.

Commas are very important in speech. If the speaker's name is written <u>before</u> the words they say, you should use a comma <u>before</u> the opening speech marks.

Matilda said, "I'd give it a good wash, Dad, if I were you, with soap and water."

If the speaker's name is written <u>after</u> the words they say, you should use a comma, a question mark or an exclamation mark <u>after</u> the speech, but <u>before</u> the closing speech marks.

"It's fabulous," Matilda said.
*"It's fabulous**!**" Matilda said.*
*"Is it fabulous**?**" Matilda said.*

Look at the sentence below, and put punctuation in the right places.

Matilda said " Please may I talk to you for a moment "

" I'm wondering what to read next " Matilda said.

" Daddy " she said " do you think you could buy me a book "

Heard you say

You can make a character sound distinctive by changing how you write their speech! Have a think about the following.

- Do they speak loudly? Quietly? Quickly? Slowly?
- Do they say a lot or not very much?
- Do they use big, clever-sounding words?
- Do they make noises that aren't words when they speak?

Matilda loves to read. Imagine she is speaking with Miss Honey about her favourite books. Continue the conversation below. Remember to use speech marks and commas, question marks or exclamation marks correctly.

"What do you like to read most, Matilda?" said Miss Honey.

Can you make your speech above sound more like Matilda and Miss Honey? Write it out again using some of the ideas on the opposite page.

HE SAID, SHE SAID

Sometimes the writer tells us what a person has said without writing it in speech marks. This is called reported speech.

Rewrite the sentences below in reported speech. Use the example answer for extra help.

"Who taught you to read, Matilda?" Miss Honey asked.

Miss Honey asked Matilda who had taught her to read.

"It's writing something!" screamed Nigel.

"What's throwing the hammer?" Lavender asked.

"Silence!" shouted the Trunchbull.

"My name is Eric Ink, Miss Trunchbull," he said.

"Am I a phenomenon?" Matilda asked.

A boy next door called Rupert Entwistle had told her that if you chopped off a newt's tail, the tail stayed alive and grew into another newt ten times bigger than the first one. It could be the size of an alligator.

Rupert told Lavender about chopping off a newt's tail. What do you think Rupert and Lavender might have said to each other? Write their conversation below.

When writing speech, always make it clear who is speaking. If a new character enters or leaves the conversation, you have to let the reader know.

When you are writing down a conversation you want to show how the person spoke, not just what they said. When Matilda says she has read the book *Nicholas Nickleby*, Miss Trunchbull does not believe her. Read the story text below.

"You are lying to me, madam!" the Trunchbull shouted, glaring at Matilda. "I doubt there is a single child in the entire school who has read that book, and here you are, an unhatched shrimp sitting in the lowest form there is, trying to tell me a whopping great lie like that!"

What adjectives, verbs or adverbs could Matilda use to describe how Miss Trunchbull spoke to her?

Adverbs describe how an action is done. For example, "she ran <u>quickly</u>."

Adjectives	**Verbs**	**Adverbs**

A whole conversation can be retold by another person. Imagine Matilda tells a friend about what Miss Trunchbull said. Write their conversation, using some of the descriptive words you wrote on the opposite page.

What they said
Pay close attention to a conversation between your friends or members of your family. Now see if you can write it all out!

READ ALL ABOUT IT!

Many people read the news in a newspaper or online every day. News articles are informative and factual, and often have a headline to catch the reader's attention.

Match the headlines to the stories below.

HOUSE TURNED UPSIDE DOWN	An ancient villa has been found underneath a car park.
ROMAN RUINS REVEALED	Footballer Lucy Lightning scores a goal in the World Cup final.
LIGHTNING STRIKES AGAIN	A boy arrives home to find his living room is upside down.

Write a headline for each of these stories.

A marvellous colourful bird goes on holiday to England.

Heavy snowfall closes all the schools in the country.

A woman has walked to the North Pole alone.

Front-page snooze

Challenge yourself! Can you make a really dull and boring story sound exciting and interesting? Have a go at writing a gripping account of these events! Remember to give them catchy headlines.

The family pet eats its breakfast.

A grown-up makes a cup of tea.

A child brushes their teeth before school.

These articles are all about made-up events. If you like, you could write an article about a real event instead. You could even start a school or family newspaper!

Newspaper stories often follow a pattern. They are written to inform the reader by answering some key questions: Who? What? When? Where? Why? Think of an interesting event or incident that has occurred recently, and then answer the questions below to plan an article about what happened.

Who?

What?

When?

Where?

Why?

Use your plan to write your own newspaper article. Don't forget the headline!

THE DAILY NEWS

In a printed newspaper, articles are usually written in columns. Do some research to find out what that looks like, and have a go yourself.

QUESTIONS AND ANSWERS

In an interview, one person asks another person lots of questions. The questions could be about the person's life, a recent event or a subject the person knows a lot about.

Interviews are often written like play-scripts, with the questions from the interviewer first, followed by the answer.

Interviewer: So, how do you feel about the giant peach, James?

James: Well, I'm absolutely thrilled! I've never seen anything like it!

Write some questions that you could ask these characters after finding the giant peach. Try to think of questions that can't be answered with just "yes" or "no".

Character	Question
James Henry Trotter	
Aunt Sponge	
Aunt Spiker	

If you're inventing interview answers for a character, imagine how their voice might sound. Complete the table below, inventing some new characters. What might they say?

Character	Notes on how they speak	Example lines
River, a talking rat		
	Uses long, complicated words Gets excited about new discoveries	
		Winning is everything! All I want to do is win!

Think of somebody to interview. It could be a character from a Roald Dahl book, another character or someone you know. Plan the interview in the space below. Use the ideas box for extra help.

What is their name?

Who are they?

What is the interview about?

Questions to ask:

Ideas box

a new Olympic running champion

an undersea explorer

a schoolboy who got stuck to a tree

Mr Centipede

a time-traveller from the future

Now write your interview.

Remember, reported speech doesn't use speech marks.

Writing an interview with a character can help you when planning a story. Asking your characters some questions helps you to think about their voice and the way they think.

INCREDIBLE INTERVIEWS

When you interview someone, you should research the person first, so you can ask them questions that are relevant to them.

Name: Miss Agatha Trunchbull
Job: Head Teacher, Crunchem Hall Primary School
Lives: The Red House, on the edge of the village
Hobbies: hammer throw
Fun fact: competed in the Olympics

What questions do you think an interviewer might want to ask the fearsome Miss Trunchbull?

Choose a few of your interview questions. Write Miss Trunchbull's answers below.

Choose one of the answers. Can you rewrite it in reported speech?

Miss Trunchbull said that

> Remember, when you interview someone you are reporting their opinions and points of view. You can ask questions to challenge their ideas, but you must never change what they say for an answer.

Imagine Matilda has been asked to interview her teacher, Miss Honey, for the local newspaper, because Miss Honey has just been voted the Nation's Best Teacher. Write the interview below and on the opposite page, using reported speech. Use the ideas box for extra help.

LOCAL TEACHER WINS TOP AWARD!

Local teacher Miss Honey has scooped the Nation's Best Teacher award aged only 23. We sent star pupil Matilda Wormwood for an exclusive interview.

Ideas box

What questions would Matilda ask?

How would Miss Honey answer?

How could Miss Honey show her emotions?

Reporting for duty

A good reporter is always ready. Grab a notepad, and fill it with a list of questions that could be used in any situation. For example:

- Why did you do that?
- What did you see and hear?
- How did that make you feel?

PERFECT PLAY-SCRIPTS

Play-scripts are written for actors to perform. They might be performed live in front of an audience, or recorded and shown later in the cinema or online. Some plays are broadcast on the radio or released as podcasts.

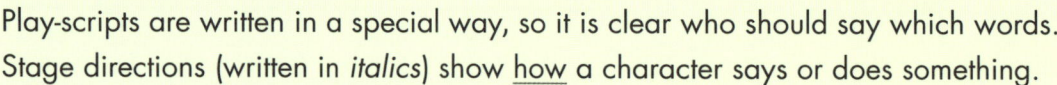

Play-scripts are written in a special way, so it is clear who should say which words. Stage directions (written in *italics*) show <u>how</u> a character says or does something.

Mr Twit: Can you feel the balloons stretching you?

Mrs Twit: I can! I can! They're stretching me like mad.

Mr Twit ties another ten balloons to Mrs Twit.

Mrs Twit *(afraid)*: Are you sure my feet are tied properly to the ground?

Look at the pictures below. What are the characters doing? How might they be speaking? Write some stage directions for each picture.

Adverbs, like "loudly" and "sadly", and adverbials, like "with a whisper" or "walking slowly", can be very useful in play-scripts. Think of some adverbs and adverbials. Write them in the space below.

> An adverbial is a word or phrase that adds more information to your writing. It can describe how, when or where something happened or was.

adverbs

giddily

adverbials

looking around

Read the sentences below, and look at the underlined words and phrases. Which are adverbs and which are adverbials?

"We most certainly wouldn't!" cried Mrs Twit. "Put some more string around my ankles <u>quickly</u>! I want to feel <u>absolutely</u> safe!"

"I'll get you for this!" shouted Mrs Twit. She was floating down <u>right on top of him</u>.

<u>Once a week, on Wednesdays</u>, the Twits had Bird Pie for supper.

Use adverbs and adverbials to complete the play-script lines below. Think carefully about how each line should be said out loud.

Mr Twit (_____): I'll wipe that silly laugh off your beaks!

Mrs Twit (_____): Now we'll never get free! We're stuck here forever!

Roly-Poly Bird (_____): You will travel by the Roly-Poly Super Jet and it won't cost you a penny!

Rewrite this passage from *The Twits* as a play-script.

"It's not the stick, it's you!" said Mr Twit, grinning horribly. *"It's you that's getting shorter! I've been noticing it for some time now."*
"That's not true!" cried Mrs Twit.
"You're shrinking, woman!" said Mr Twit.
"It's not possible!"

Mr Twit (grinning horribly):

Ideas box
Can you read out your script with a friend? You could even try it on your own, doing different voices for Mr and Mrs Twit!

Don't forget to include your stage directions. What might your characters be doing? They could be waggling a finger, dancing on the spot or running off the stage completely!

Put on a show
Once you have rehearsed your script, you need to perform it! Think about all the other elements that will make a good play. You might want to think about:

- costumes
- make-up
- music
- stage directions.

THROUGH EACH OTHER'S EYES

When you are reading a newspaper article, the writer might have used descriptive words that tell you what they think about the people in the article. You might agree with the writer's opinion, or you might disagree!

"He's barmy!" they shouted.
"He's nutty!"
"He's screwy!"
"He's batty!"
"He's dippy!"
"He's dotty!"
"He's daffy!"
"He's goofy!"
"He's beany!"
"He's buggy!"
"He's wacky!"
"He's loony!"
"No, he is not!" said Grandpa Joe.

The parents describe Willy Wonka in synonyms, or words with similar meanings. But Grandpa Joe says Willy Wonka is brilliant. How many synonyms can you think of for "brilliant"?

wonderful

brilliant

The other side
Grandpa Joe thinks Willy Wonka is brilliant. Does Mr Slugworth, Mr Wonka's rival, feel the same? Once you've written down your synonyms, have a go at coming up with words for someone who feels the opposite way.

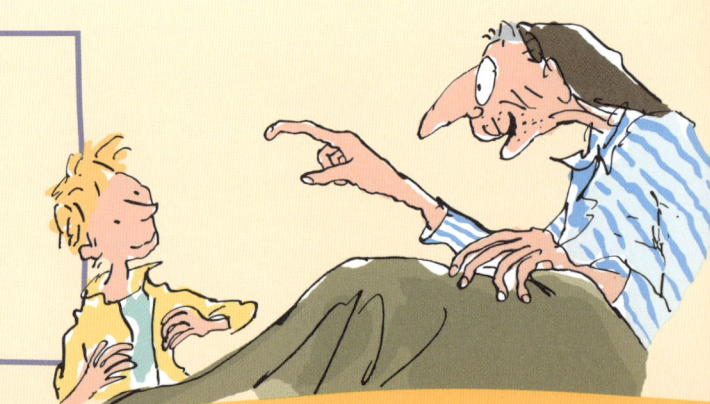

The synonym "beany" is completely invented. Think of six words to describe Willy Wonka – three real ones and three invented ones.

Real	**Invented**

How might Grandpa Joe describe Willy Wonka? Write his description below. You can use synonyms and maybe even some invented words!

> To invent a new word, try combining words that have the same meaning. It will make your new word easier to understand.

Several of the children in *Charlie and the Chocolate Factory* are introduced in the newspaper, such as Veruca Salt. Charlie's grandparents think they don't sound very nice. Look at the family's reactions below, and circle any words that show their opinions of the children.

"What a repulsive boy," said Grandma Georgina.

"Do all children behave like this nowadays – like these brats we've been hearing about?"

"Beastly girl," said Grandma Josephine.

Imagine you are a news reporter. What would you write about Charlie after he finds his Golden Ticket? What words would you use to describe him? Plan your ideas in the space below.

Write your news article, using the ideas box for extra help.

FINAL TICKET FINDER!

Ideas box

You could include:

- an interview with Charlie's mother
- quotes from his grandparents
- Charlie's own reaction
- that this is the last Golden ticket

YOU ARE A WRITER!

This is a chance for you to use one of the reasons to write that you've learned about in this book. Write one more trick for Mr Twit to play on Mrs Twit!

Amazing! Splendid! Stupendous! Magnificent! You did it! You made it! You should feel so proud of yourself!

Plan the trick in the space below. You can write and draw what happens.

Which reason to write will help you to describe the trick? Circle the type of writing you are going to produce.

Instructions for the trick

An interview after the trick took place

A newspaper report about what happened

Mrs Twit's diary for the day of the trick

84

Now write about the trick using the type of writing you chose on the opposite page.

> Many professional writers keep a notepad and pen with them all the time. You never know when a good idea will come to you!

TIME TO PLAN YOUR WRITING!

No matter what format you want to use to share your information, it's important to plan what you want to write.

Think of an idea or some information you'd like to share with people. Use the boxes below to plan out the best format to share your writing in, and how you will write it.

If you need more space for your ideas, you can copy these boxes out on to more paper or into a notepad.

1
Idea

2
Type(s) of writing

3
Beginning

4
Middle

5
End

MY REMARKABLE REASONS TO WRITE

Use the balloons on the following pages to plan your ideas for each different type of writing. Then practise writing, using your new skills!

A story based on real events

First

Then

Next

After that

Finally

Remember, the most important reasons to write anything are because:
- you want to!
- you enjoy it!

A newspaper article

Who?
What?
When?
Where?
Why?

An interview

Questions

Instructions

First

Next

Finally

A letter

Formal   Informal

A diary entry

Events   Feelings   Thoughts

A recipe

Ingredients

Instructions